CODING CAREERS
IN THE MILITARY

Kate Shoup

Cavendish
Square

New York

Published in 2020 by Cavendish Square Publishing, LLC
243 5th Avenue, Suite 136, New York, NY 10016

Library of Congress Cataloging-in-Publication Data

Names: Shoup, Kate, 1972- author.
Title: Coding careers in the military / Kate Shoup.
Description: First edition. | New York : Cavendish Square, [2020] |
Series: Coding careers for tomorrow | Includes bibliographical references and index. |
Audience: Grades 7-12. Identifiers: LCCN 2019003076 (print) | LCCN 2019004114 (ebook) |
ISBN 9781502645890 (ebook) | ISBN 9781502645883 (library bound) |
ISBN 9781502645876 (pbk.) Subjects: LCSH: United States–Armed Forces–Vocational guidance–
Juvenile literature. | Computer programming–Vocational guidance–Juvenile literature.
Classification: LCC UB147 (ebook) | LCC UB147 .S55 2020 (print) |
DDC 355.0023/73–dc23 LC record available at https://lccn.loc.gov/2019003076

Editorial Director: David McNamara
Editor: Kristen Susienka
Copy Editor: Denise Larrabee
Associate Art Director: Alan Sliwinski
Designer: Ginny Kemmerer
Production Coordinator: Karol Szymczuk
Photo Research: J8 Media

The photographs in this book are used by permission and through the courtesy of: Cover Aleksei
Gorodenkov/Alamy Stock Photo, background (and used throughout the book) Maciek905/iStockphoto.
com; p. 4 Smederevac/iStock/Getty Images; p. 6 Best Backgrounds/Shutterstock.com; p. 8 Bettmann/Getty
Images, background (and used throughout the book) MF3d/iStockphoto.com; p. 11 Massoud Hossaini/
AFP/Getty Images; p. 12 Tech. Sgt. Richard Ebensberger/U.S. Air Force/DVIDS; p. 16 Apic/Getty Images;
p. 20 Andreas Feininger/The LIFE Picture Collection/Getty Images; p. 22 Sovfoto/UIG/Getty Images; p.
24 Brooks Kraft LLC/Sygma/Getty Images; p. 28 Koto Feja/iStock/Getty Images; p. 32 Joseph Eddins,
Jr./U.S. Air Force/DVIDS; p. 34 Photo12/UIG/Getty Images; p. 36 Senior Airman Kenneth Norman/U.S.
Air Force/DVIDS; p. 37 Airman 1st Class Samuel Contreras/U.S. Air Force/DVIDS; p. 40 Seth Wenig/AP
Images; p. 44 Alun Thomas/Mike Scheck, USAREC Public Affairs/DVIDS; p. 47 Andrew Harrer/Bloomberg/
Getty Images; p. 48 Gorodenkoff/Shutterstock.com; p. 51 United States Cyber Command/Wikimedia
Commons/File:Seal of the United States Cyber Command.svg/Public Domain; p. 54 Trevor Tiernan/U.S.
Air Force/DVIDS; p. 56 Jim West/Alamy Stock Photo; p. 63 Monkey Business Images/Shutterstock.com;
p. 64 Hero Images/Getty Images; p. 66 Maya/E+/Getty Images; p. 67 Martin Bureau/AFP/Getty Images.

Printed in the United States of America

Contents

Lots of computer coders work for the military.

chapter_01

All About
Military Coding Jobs

A computer coder—also called a computer programmer or a software developer—is someone who designs and builds computer programs to follow a certain set of tasks. Today there are millions of computer programs designed to do all sorts of things. Another word for computer program is software. Computer coding used to be a special skill that few people knew how to do. Today it is as important to learn as reading, writing, or math.

HOW COMPUTER PROGRAMS ARE BUILT

Until the 1970s, computer coders used thick pieces of paper called punch cards to build computer programs. First the coder wrote out the program's data and instructions. Then, for each piece of data or program instruction, the coder punched a set pattern of holes into a punch card. A program might require hundreds or even thousands of these cards in order for it to work. The complete set of cards for a program was called the source deck.

After the coder completed the source deck for a program, it was fed into a special machine called a compiler. The compiler "translated" the data and program instructions into a special language that a computer could read. This is called machine language. The result was a new stack of cards with holes punched through them. This was called the program deck. This was the actual program. To perform the

Coders write computer code by typing programming commands into a text file. This is an example of computer code.

task that the program was built to complete, a computer operator inserted the program deck into a computer, which processed the cards.

Today, coders no longer use punch cards to build programs, but many of the ideas and terms that helped create the first computer programs are still used. Programmers use one of several programming languages to type program instructions into a computer text file. These instructions are called the source code. Next, coders run their source code through a special computer program called a compiler. As with the compiler machines of old, modern compilers "translate" the source code into a machine language that a computer can read, called object code. (Some source code is designed to skip this step. This code is said to be *interpreted*.) This object code consists of a series of zeroes and ones, whose order dictates how the program will behave.

There are thousands of programming languages, each with their own characteristics. Some of these are called low-level languages. Low-level languages are similar to machine language. As such, these languages are harder for humans to read and learn. Other languages are called high-level languages. High-level languages have a set structure and often use words found in human languages. They might also automate certain programming functions. This makes them easier to learn and use.

Grace Hopper: Computer Pioneer

Here, Grace Hopper writes a program on punch tape, which will then be fed into a calculating machine.

A US Navy officer named Grace Hopper invented the first computer language in 1953. The language was called Common Business-Oriented Language (COBOL). It was more similar to English than the machine language used by computers. This made it easier for computer coders to learn. Hopper also came up with the term "bug" after a moth got sucked into a computer she was working on and caused the system to crash.

Hopper was born in 1906 in New York City. In 1934, she earned a PhD in mathematics from Yale University. She taught mathematics at Vassar College. During World War II, Hopper joined the US Navy Reserves. She was assigned the role of computer programmer and learned how to code.

After the war, Hopper continued to serve in the Navy Reserves. She also accepted a job at a computer company called the Eckert-Mauchly Computer Corporation (EMCC). In those days, computers didn't look like they do now. They took up whole rooms! While working at EMCC, Hopper invented COBOL. She also helped build the first computer available for sale to the public. It was called the UNIVAC I.

Hopper retired from the Navy Reserves in 1946. However, the Navy recalled her to active duty the next year. Hopper remained in the Navy until 1986. She achieved the rank of rear admiral. After Hopper's death in 1992, the US Navy named a ship after her: the USS *Hopper*. Hopper also received the National Medal of Technology and Innovation and the Presidential Medal of Freedom. Hopper was a real computer pioneer!

Programming languages have other characteristics. Some are general-purpose, while others are meant for a specific use; some are imperative (that is, containing a sequence of specific operations to perform in order to gain a desired outcome), while some are declarative (meaning they specify the desired result but not the steps needed to achieve it); and so on.

COMPUTERS AND THE MILITARY

The first computers were called analog computers. Analog computers have existed in one form or another since ancient times. Each analog computer was designed to perform a specific type of calculation using a mechanical or electrical model. An analog computer could not be reprogrammed to perform a different calculation.

During World War II, the US military built one of the world's first digital computers. Digital computers were faster and more flexible than analog computers. Some early digital computers performed complex calculations. Others stored data about individual soldiers, such as their location and status.

Today the US military uses computers to handle all sorts of tasks. Some of these are administrative tasks, such as managing supplies and issuing paychecks. Others include handling communications, analyzing and organizing intelligence and other data, pinpointing locations, running training simulations, and administering health care.

Modern military computers are also used to fight wars. For example, the military uses computers with special software to control weapons such as missiles and drones. This helps keep US troops out of harm's way.

Sometimes computers and software *are* the weapons. This is the case with cyber warfare. Cyber warfare is a new way of fighting that involves breaking into an enemy's computer systems to spy on them, to cause damage, or to shut them down.

This unmanned drone carries a missle. It is stationed at Kandahar Airfield in Afghanistan in 2010.

The US military has four main branches: the US Army, US Navy, US Air Force, and US Marine Corps. There is also a US Coast Guard. People who work in these five branches are said to be enlisted. Then there is the Army National Guard and the Air National Guard. People who work in these two branches are called reserves. They work part time and serve as backup for enlisted troops in the main military branches. All branches of the military are part of the US Department

Military aircraft rely heavily on computers. Here, a military pilot reviews computer data inside the cockpit of an aircraft at the Dyess Air Force Base in Abilene, Texas.

of Defense. The Department of Defense is sometimes called the DoD or the Pentagon.

The Department of Defense and the different branches of the military use different types of computers and computer programs. For example, sailors in the Navy and Coast Guard use special computer programs to navigate ships, pilots in the Navy and Air Force use different computer systems to fly fighter jets, and so on. The software found in the computer system for one US fighter jet called the F35 Joint Strike Fighter contains more than twenty-four million lines of code!

Many computer programs are built by the Department of Defense or the military for its own use. Sometimes the people who write the code for these programs work for the Department of Defense or serve in the military. More often these programs are coded by people who work for companies hired by the military or the Department of Defense. These companies and the people who work for them are called defense contractors, military contractors, or sometimes simply civilians.

MODERN MILITARY COMPUTER SYSTEMS

Computer coding is an important job. This is especially true in the military. "Software is becoming the pivotal element behind weapons and information systems, and is increasingly the thing that will determine who has the upper hand," says journalist Mark Wallace.

However, military coders don't just focus on these types of systems. They also build and maintain systems for the following types of tasks:

ADMINISTRATION: Like any large organization, the Department of Defense and each branch of the military must perform certain administrative tasks—managing supplies and personnel, handling payroll, and more. Many military coders build systems and programs to complete these tasks.

COMMUNICATION: The military depends on a complex communication network to relay critical information both on and off the battlefield. This network is built from a variety of computers, devices, and programs.

INTELLIGENCE: Some military computer systems are designed to gather and analyze intelligence data. This data could come from various sources, such as drone video footage, enemy activity on the internet, or human beings on the ground.

NAVIGATION: The military relies heavily on computerized navigation systems to guide troops to their targets.

TRAINING: Members of the military use computers to train for all types of jobs. Military computer training programs range from simple guided courses to full-scale simulations such as flight or combat simulations. Some of these are similar to video games.

HEALTH CARE: The military provides health-care services for troops on active duty as well as for veterans who have retired from the military. This involves the use of a variety of computers and devices that use special software.

Simply put, the Department of Defense and the military need coders to build and maintain all sorts of tasks. There's no reason you can't be one of them!

Computer programmers work alongside the famous ENIAC computer in 1946.

chapter_02

Coding Changes the Military and the World

The US military has used computers for decades. However, at first, these "computers" were simply people who performed complex mathematical calculations using their brains.

In the beginning, the primary task of many human military computers was to calculate the trajectories of different types of artillery—that is, the path and distance of a particular shell fired from a particular gun in a particular set of conditions. Fighters on ships, airplanes, and tanks needed this information to aim their weapons correctly. There was just one problem: it took a human computer as long as forty hours to calculate a single trajectory.

EARLY MILITARY COMPUTER SYSTEMS: ENIAC AND SAGE

During World War II, the US Army needed a quicker way to calculate these trajectories. Army officials hired two professors from the University of Pennsylvania, John Mauchly and J. Presper Eckert, to build and program a digital computer to do the job. This computer was called the Electronic Numerical Integrator and Computer (ENIAC).

ENIAC was completed in the fall of 1945. It was among the first electronic digital computers ever constructed—after the German Z3 (completed in 1941) and the British Colossus (finished in 1943). It bore little resemblance to computers today. It weighed 27 tons (25 metric tons) and filled an entire room. It used enough electricity in one second to power a typical home for more than a week. And it could run only one program at a time. Running a different program meant completely rewiring the machine. This process took a team of programmers as long as two days. (Interestingly, many of these programmers were women.)

By the fall of 1945, when Mauchly and Eckert finished building ENIAC, the war had ended—so it was never used for its original purpose: to calculate shell trajectories (although it could do so in just twenty seconds). However, ENIAC didn't go to waste. The scientists who developed the first hydrogen bomb used ENIAC to test their early designs. The director of that effort wrote in 1946 that "the complexity of these problems is so great that it would have been impossible to arrive at any solution without the aid of ENIAC."

After World War II, the United States soon found itself in another conflict, the Cold War. Its enemy was the Soviet Union. Many Americans feared the Soviet Union would attack the United States. The Soviet Union was expanding its cache of powerful atomic weapons. The United States wanted to be prepared, so they also made more technological advances. They developed computers, stronger weapons, and other defense and warfare technologies. However, it was hoped that these weapons would never actually be used. "The Cold War was waged on political, economic, and propaganda fronts and had only limited recourse to weapons," says the *Encyclopedia Britannica.*

As part of the effort to protect against a Soviet attack, the US military built an air-defense system called the Semi-Automatic Ground Environment (SAGE). According to a 1953 memo, the SAGE system consisted of "(1) a net of radars and other data sources and (2) digital computers that (a) receive the radar and other information to detect and track aircraft, (b) process the track data to form a complete air situation, and (c) guide weapons to destroy enemy aircraft." The backbone of the SAGE system was a special computer called the AN/FSQ-7. It was built by a company called International Business Machines (IBM). Each AN/FSQ-7 machine weighed 250 tons (227 metric tons) and

IBM's AN/FSQ-7 machines were used to protect the United States against a Soviet attack. This image shows two men working on one of the machines.

occupied half an acre (0.2 hectares) of floor space. There were more than fifty of these machines.

The AN/FSQ-7 machines ran software that contained more than half a million lines of code. According to the Lincoln Laboratory at the Massachusetts Institute of Technology (MIT), where much of the work on SAGE was completed, "The art of computer programming was essentially invented for SAGE."

Soon the US military was using computers for many purposes. Professor Paul N. Edwards writes:

Built directly into weapons systems, computers assisted or replaced human skill in aiming and operating advanced weapons, such as antiaircraft guns and missiles. They automated the calculation of tables. They solved difficult mathematical problems in weapons engineering and in the scientific research behind military technologies, augmenting or replacing human calculation.

To perform these and other tasks, computers used complex computer programs. Each of these programs was built by military coders.

THE DEFENSE ADVANCED RESEARCH PROJECTS AGENCY (DARPA)

In 1957, the Soviet Union launched *Sputnik 1*. It was the first satellite ever sent into space. Although *Sputnik 1* was not a weapon, its launch scared many Americans. They worried the Soviet Union had become more technologically advanced than the United States. This could give the Soviets a decisive edge in the ongoing Cold War.

In response to *Sputnik 1*, US President Dwight D. Eisenhower formed a special government agency to develop new military technologies, including computer technologies. This agency was called the Advanced Research Projects Agency (ARPA). Later its name changed to the Defense

This is *Sputnik 1*. Its launch by the Soviet Union prompted the United States to form ARPA (later called DARPA), which eventually changed the technological world forever.

Advanced Research Projects Agency (DARPA). DARPA is still part of the Department of Defense today.

Since its beginning, DARPA has employed computer coders (and others) to develop a variety of advanced technologies for military use. One example of these technologies is precision weapons. These are missiles that use computers to pinpoint their target. Another example is the Global Positioning System (GPS). It was developed for navigation purposes.

DARPA was also behind the development of the modern internet. At first the network, originally called the ARPANET, consisted of just four linked computers—three in California and one in Utah. Today the internet connects billions of computers around the globe. More recently, DARPA has conducted important research in the areas of artificial intelligence (AI) and machine learning (ML), robotics, and cybersecurity. AI describes when a machine displays intelligence; ML refers to the algorithms and models used by machines to learn through experience over time. Computer coders have played key roles in all these DARPA research efforts.

THE IMPACT OF COMPUTER TECHNOLOGY ON THE NATURE OF WARFARE

"New technologies have always shaped the ways we go to war," writes journalist Mark Wallace. This was true when our ancestors switched from simple weapons like rocks, spears, daggers, and swords to more complex ones like catapults, crossbows, guns, gas, and bombs. And it's true today as we begin to use computers in warfare.

One obvious way computers have shaped the nature of warfare is by speeding up the process of analyzing and communicating critical data. This gives fighters the information they need to quickly make the best possible decisions. More and more, what will make a difference in warfare will be whether the military's high-functioning computers are strong and fast enough to process larger amounts of information.

Computers have also brought about entirely new forms of warfare. One of these is cyber warfare. Cyber warfare involves using malware as a weapon to disable the computer systems of an enemy. Malware is short for malicious software. Malware is designed to damage or exploit a computer system.

Recent years have seen an increase in cyber warfare attacks. An example of such an attack occurred in 2017 when Russian hackers allegedly released a virus—a type of malware designed to disable any system it infects—that targeted computers in Ukraine. This opened a "new era of warfare" that involves "undermining democracy, wrecking livelihoods by targeting critical infrastructure and weaponizing

Modern fighters use computers on the battlefield. Here, US troops test equipment and computers at Fort Irwin training center in California.

THE "ELECTRONIC BATTLEFIELD"

In 1969, US Army General William C. Westmoreland described what he called "the battlefield of the future." On this battlefield, he said, "enemy forces will be located, tracked, and targeted almost instantaneously through the use of data-links, computer-assisted intelligence evaluation and automated fire control." He called this the electronic battlefield.

Westmoreland's vision has become a reality. Thanks to computer systems, and the people who code them, the US military can mobilize more quickly, with less risk, and at a lower cost than ever before. Indeed, says historian Williamson Murray, "The ground forces of the United States are dependent on technological and space-based systems to execute their most basic tasks on the battlefield." Murray continues, "This is also true to an even greater extent for navy and air force."

However, to quote one army official, "capabilities create dependencies and dependencies create vulnerabilities." In other words, even as technology makes the military stronger, its *dependence* on technology creates a weakness. This is because technology is vulnerable to attack by hackers and cyberterrorists.

Fortunately, computer coders can help protect military computers by writing secure code and by implementing other cybersecurity measures.

information," said British defense secretary Gavin Williamson after the attack.

The United States has also engaged in cyber warfare. An example of this was the Stuxnet worm. A worm is like a virus but spreads in a different way. This Stuxnet worm was discovered in 2010. It was allegedly coded by Israeli and American cyber warriors. A cyber warrior is someone who builds malware, such as viruses or worms, for use in cyber warfare. Security experts say the worm infected computers in Iran that operated that country's nuclear centrifuges. American cyber warriors also allegedly infected computers in North Korea in 2014 to sabotage its missile program.

Experts have grown increasingly worried that cyber warfare could lead to real-world warfare. "The first shots of the next actual war will likely be fired in cyberspace," says Army General Mark Milley.

In addition to cyber warfare, developments in computer technology have resulted in drone warfare. A drone is like a flying robot: an aircraft with no pilot inside. Drones operate using software programmed by computer coders. Some drones are remote controlled via computer by an operator on the ground—sometimes thousands of miles away. Other drones are autonomous. While most drones are programmed for surveillance purposes, some engage in direct warfare, shooting missiles at specific targets.

In recent years, the US military has relied on drones in its efforts to combat terrorism. "Drones have devastated al Qaeda and associated anti-American militant groups," a Washington-based think tank called the Brookings Institution wrote in 2013. "And they have done so at little financial cost, at no risk to US forces, and with fewer civilian casualties than many alternative methods would have caused."

Finally, advances in computer technology have led to developing new weapons that involve artificial intelligence and machine learning. Weapons that use AI and ML are often called autonomous weapons because they can work mostly without control by people. An example of an AI weapon is a missile that contains software that enables it to choose between multiple targets.

Some people are nervous about autonomous weapons. In 2015, prominent figures like Elon Musk, Stephen Hawking, Steve Wozniak, and thousands of scientific researchers signed an open letter to ban their use. "If any major military power pushes ahead with AI weapon development," the letter said, "a global arms race is virtually inevitable." If these weapons were to fall into the wrong hands, they could easily be used "for tasks such as assassinations, destabilizing nations, subduing populations and selectively killing a particular ethnic group." Therefore, the letter concluded, an "AI arms race would not be beneficial for humanity."

THE DOWNSIDES OF DRONE WARFARE

Drone warfare has pros and cons. They can be used to target specific places without putting soldiers' lives at risk, but sometimes they can cause unwanted deaths and destruction near the areas they target.

The use of drones helps prevent casualties among US troops and local civilians. However, drones have their critics. Some critics say that the use of drones causes resentment among civilians in targeted areas. "Drone strikes may be an efficient way to kill terrorists," observes journalist Doyle McManus. "But they're no way to make friends." Critics also suggest that conducting drone attacks is too easy—like playing a video game. This may prevent drone operators from making ethical decisions when conducting a strike. Finally, some critics question the legality of drone strikes.

Drone warfare also takes a toll on drone operators. "Their work carries its own set of psychological stressors," National Public Radio (NPR) reports. Even though they may be thousands of miles away from the strike, drone operators must watch as the deadly events unfold. Sometimes they must even decide who lives and who dies. For some, this can be traumatic. NPR explains: "Observing the horrors of war, over and over again—even from a distance—carries a heavy burden." Fortunately, the military is aware of this problem and has begun taking steps to help drone operators cope.

However, AI *could* be put to good military use in other ways. For example, it could be employed for the purposes of cyber security, to handle logistics, to improve health care on the battlefield, for simulation purposes, to quickly process large quantities of data, and more.

THE EFFECTS OF MILITARY CODERS ON AMERICAN SOCIETY

"From the early 1940s until the early 1960s," says professor Paul N. Edwards, "the armed forces of the United States were the single most important driver of digital computer development." However, for the most part, the military didn't design and build computers itself. Instead, it hired university researchers and tech companies to perform these tasks. (This is called outsourcing.) Consequently, the US military in general and the SAGE program in particular "became a driving force behind the formation of the American computer and electronics industry" and initiated "the digital computing revolution that has had such a significant impact on today's world," says the MIT Lincoln Laboratory.

This digital revolution didn't happen overnight. During the 1960s, the technology companies founded to build computers for the military began selling them to large corporations to handle business tasks like managing inventory and payroll, storing files, and producing reports. During the 1980s, technology companies began building personal computers (PCs) and selling them to regular consumers. During the 1990s, the internet and related software like web browsers and email programs became available for the general public to use.

This explosion in the use of computers has led to dramatic changes in society today. "Computers have changed the way people relate to one another and their living environment, as well as how humans organize their work, their communities, and their time," says computer researcher William McIver Jr.

None of this could have happened without the computer coders who worked on early military computers like ENIAC and other projects paid for by the US Department of Defense during World War II and the Cold War—or certainly not as quickly. "Without the vast research funding and the atmosphere of desperation associated with the war," observes Professor Edwards, "it probably would have been years, perhaps decades, before private industry attempted" a project like ENIAC. Simply put, says author Frank Rose, "The computerization of society has essentially been a side effect of the computerization of war."

Staff Sergeant Jamie Benites (*left*) and Major Drew Armstrong (*right*) discuss a US Department of Defense software development project.

chapter_03

Challenges and Technologies

Coders who work in the US Department of Defense, the military, or for a military contractor have a few unique challenges. One is that although the Department of Defense was the driving force behind the development of early computer technologies, it has since fallen behind in some areas. In fact, some military and Department of Defense facilities use computers that might be better placed in a museum. According to one former US congressman, "the federal government"—including certain computer systems within the Department of Defense and the military—"is years, sometimes decades, behind the private sector."

CHALLENGES FACING MILITARY CODERS

A 2016 report by the US General Accounting Office (GAO) revealed that several systems used by the Pentagon were decades old. One such system is the Strategic Automated Command and Control System. This system is responsible for coordinating "the operational functions of the United States' nuclear forces, such as intercontinental ballistic missiles, nuclear bombers, and tanker support aircrafts," says the GAO. It runs on computers from the 1970s and relies on old 8-inch (20.3-centimenter) floppy disks to store information. Fortunately, this system is slated for replacement by the end of 2020.

In addition to using outdated equipment, many Department of Defense and military systems are coded with outmoded programming languages. An example of this is the Defense

English painter Margaret Sarah Carpenter created this image of Ada Lovelace in 1836.

Joint Military Pay System (DJMPS). This system is used to pay members of the military. It was coded using COBOL, which was invented in the 1950s. Other military systems were built using a language called Ada. This programming language was named for Ada Lovelace. She is credited as the first person ever to write a computer program, in 1843. The computer language Ada was developed during the early 1980s by coders hired by the Pentagon. It was meant to standardize code used in certain military computer systems. In 1991, the US Congress passed a law requiring its use in all Department of Defense software—including military software. However, this law is no longer in effect.

To complicate matters, computer systems maintained by the Pentagon and various military branches are rarely compatible. "None of it plays well together," says journalist Mark Wallace. He explains: "Data from a Patriot missile radar, for instance, can be used to aim and launch Patriot missiles, but is generally unavailable to other weapons systems that might be able to use it to enhance the nation's defense."

A NEW DIRECTION

There's a movement afoot to promote innovation in military technology. This is part of a new military strategy called the Third Offset Strategy. According to former Deputy Defense Secretary Bob Work, the Third Offset strategy puts special emphasis on technologies like artificial intelligence

One piece of the Third Offset Strategy is to enable troops to use personal electronics to share tactical information. This image shows troops using smartphones at an air force base in South Carolina in 2014.

—"particularly in things like cyber defense, electronic warfare defense, [and] missile defense." It also seeks to enable troops to use personal electronics like smartphones and other devices to share tactical information; use big data—extremely large sets of data that can be analyzed to spot patterns and trends—to track terrorist activities; use technology to help with decision-making; and more.

To help put this new military strategy into place, the Department of Defense has created two new divisions, the Defense Innovation Unit Experimental (DIUx) and the Strategic Capabilities Office (SCO). "DIUx is specifically charged with talking and working with the tech sector in Silicon Valley, Boston and Austin," says DefenseNews. Meanwhile, "SCO is charged with taking existing technologies and developing new capabilities for their use."

The Department of Defense has also established a special Defense Innovation Board (DIB) to advise the secretary of defense on technology matters. Members of the board include executives at tech companies and researchers from top universities. Key areas of focus include "artificial intelligence and machine learning, software workforce capacity building, hiring and retention of I+STEM talent, acquisition reform, communication networks, IT infrastructure, and working with the tech industry," says the DIB's website.

In addition to pushing for the development of new technologies like artificial intelligence, the Pentagon and

This soldier tests out virtual reality aviation software in a new innovation lab at Maxwell Air Force Base in Alabama in 2018.

various military branches are also working to improve how these technologies are conceived, built, and used. This has resulted in a new set of software standards called the Open Mission Systems (OMS) architecture. The OMS architecture allows the military to design and build systems that can be easily modified. So, for example, "instead of spending more than $200 million on an aircraft that can do one thing," says journalist Mark Wallace, the military can purchase a "multipurpose 'smartplane' that can be quickly repurposed to fly a variety of missions, that can integrate new technologies with minimum effort, and which can provide data that a variety of military systems can consume."

There has also been a push to use open source software within the Department of Defense for certain types of programs. There's even a special group within the department that promotes its use: the Military Open Source Software Working Group (Mil-OSS). Open source software is software whose source code is available to the general public to study or even modify. Open source software has three big advantages. First, it is usually free. Second, it tends to improve more quickly than closed software. (Closed software is software whose code is kept secret by the person or organization that wrote it.) And third, it is almost always stronger and more secure than closed software. Of course, not *all* Department of Defense programs would be built using open source. Code for critical systems "used for spying, encryption and decryption, relaying commands, or directing weapons" would not be shared or publicized, says journalist Kelsey Atherton.

Finally, the Pentagon has begun exploring the use of cloud computing. Cloud computing involves storing and accessing data and programs over the internet. "Accelerating [the Department of Defense's] adoption of cloud computing is critical to maintaining our military's technical advantage," Deputy Defense Secretary Patrick M. Shanahan said in 2017. Cloud computing is cheaper and more secure than traditional computer systems. Furthermore, information stored on the cloud can be made readily available to anyone who needs it and is authorized to access it. The bottom line, according to Nancy A. Norton, director of the Defense Information Systems Agency: "The cloud will simplify and provide flexibility to the way [the Department of Defense] works with information that's secure."

All these developments mean one thing: the Pentagon, the military, and the contractors who work with them will need lots of smart computer coders!

USEFUL PROGRAMMING LANGUAGES FOR MILITARY CODERS

Military coders need not study every programming language. That would be impossible. There are thousands of programming languages in use throughout the world.

THE PROMISE OF
QUANTUM COMPUTING

This is what IBM's quantum computer looks like.

For the last several years, scientists have been working on a new kind of computer called a quantum computer. Quantum computers use principles of quantum physics to process information much more quickly than their traditional counterparts.

In 2018, the Department of Defense prioritized research into quantum computing. Defense officials say quantum computers could allow the military to quickly perform computations that are too complex for traditional computers, crack "unbreakable" codes, calculate ML algorithms for AI machines, establish completely secure lines of communication, and more.

Constructing a quantum computer that is more powerful than a traditional machine has been difficult for several reasons. First, quantum computing is a very new field; only a few quantum programming languages exist, and not many people know them. Examples of such languages are Quantum Computer Language (QCL), Q# (pronounced Q-sharp), and Quipper. Coders who learn these or other quantum languages will have a leg up as quantum computing takes off!

Despite difficulty in advancing this technology, IBM has made some headway developing a quantum computer. Also, Chinese scientists say they're on track to build one that can compete with the world's most powerful supercomputer in 2020. That means the US military will need to work hard to maintain its technological edge—and they'll need coders who understand quantum computing to do it.

However, there are a few languages that military coders should learn—depending on what area of the Department of Defense or military they work in or with and on what type of system. These include the following:

COBOL: COBOL may be an outmoded programming language, but many military systems still use it, and likely will for some time. "In many cases ... maintaining an older system that fully supports our mission makes more sense than upgrading it or buying a new system that runs the risk of degrading our mission and requires a large investment," observed Terry Halvorsen of the Department of Defense in 2014. That means coders who know COBOL will remain in demand in the military.

ADA: It used to be that all military programs were required by law to be coded using Ada. That's no longer the case. However, as with COBOL, plenty of military systems still use it—meaning there's a demand for coders who know it.

C AND C++: C was developed during the 1970s and remains a popular general-purpose programming language. C++ (pronounced C-plus-plus) is an updated version of C. It compiles more quickly and provides better overall performance.

HTML: HTML is used to build simple websites. This language is very easy to learn.

JAVA: Released in 1995, Java was the first computer language that allowed computers on different patforms such as Microsoft Windows and Apple Macintosh to communicate with each other. Thanks to this flexibility, Java has been used to program web applications, mobile devices, supercomputers—even NASA's Mars rovers! Many military contractors continue to use Java for various projects.

JAVASCRIPT: Based on its name, JavaScript seems like it would be an offshoot of Java. However, it isn't. It's a special kind of language called a scripting language. The purpose of a scripting language is to make a web page more animated or interactive. For example, coders might use a scripting language like JavaScript to embed video content into a web page. JavaScript is very popular. It appears in the source code for most modern websites.

PYTHON: Programmers often call Python the Swiss Army knife of programming languages. This is because it can be used for many different purposes—including for AI programs. As a bonus, Python is very easy to learn.

Don't limit yourself to learning just one of these languages. The more languages you know, the more valuable you will be as a military coder!

Enlisting in the military can open up a wealth of opportunities for aspiring computer coders. These men and women are seen enlisting at a recruiting event in 2017.

chapter_04

Coding Career Possibilities

Throughout America there is a growing demand for computer coders. According to the US Bureau of Labor Statistics, there will be a 24 percent increase in the number of computer-coding jobs between 2016 and 2026. These are good, high-paying jobs, with a median salary of more than $100,000 per year. However, so far it looks like there won't be enough coders to fill them.

CODERS ARE IN DEMAND!

It's not just companies that need these coders. It's the US government too—including the Department of Defense, the military, and the contractors who work with them. Indeed, coders and other computer-savvy types "are in high demand

and short supply all across the Pentagon," says journalist Joe Pappalardo. This means young people interested in becoming military coders have a bright future indeed!

COOL JOBS FOR MILITARY CODERS

Most military coding jobs involve building code to help maintain and update systems for the Department of Defense and the military. People who do these jobs are often called computer systems programmers. "These experts write, analyze, design and develop programs that are critical to our war-fighting capabilities," according to one job posting for a computer systems programming position in the US Air Force. "From maintenance tracking programs to programs that organize and display intelligence data, they ensure we have the software and programs needed to complete our missions efficiently and effectively." This job requires only that applicants have a high school degree (or equivalent) and enlist in the Air Force; applicants selected by the Air Force are trained on the job.

Some military coding jobs are more specific, such as cybersecurity specialist. A cybersecurity specialist protects military computers against cyber terrorists and other threats, such as malware. Experts predict that in the coming years, the US federal government—including the Department of Defense and the military—will have a severe shortage of these specialists. This will put the nation at greater risk of cyberattacks by terrorists, spies, and criminals. As one security expert put it, "The greatest virtual threat today is not state-sponsored cyberattacks, newfangled clandestine malware, or a hacker culture run amok. The most dangerous looming crisis … is instead a severe cybersecurity labor shortage." It will be up to coders employed by the Department of Defense, the military, and the contractors that work with them to combat this growing threat.

In addition to these, there are countless other types of military coding jobs. For example, some of these jobs involve coding simulation programs. These programs are similar to video games and simulate activities like flying a fighter jet or engaging in combat. They are used to train military personnel.

These coders are working hard at the Department of Defense.

Cyber warriors are the newest type of fighter. There are many opportunities to help this area grow.

Some cybersecurity specialists are cyber warriors. Remember, cyber warriors engage in cyber warfare by building viruses, worms, or other malware. The purpose of this malware is to infect the computer systems of America's enemies.

Many coders who work in cyber warfare must have a security clearance. A security clearance gives the holder access to confidential or even classified information.

Cyber warfare is controversial. Critics at *Foreign Policy* magazine say cyber warfare attacks can "cause collateral damage far beyond the original, intended target." This was the case with the NotPetya virus allegedly released by Russian operatives in 2017. In addition to crippling target systems in Ukraine, this virus caused billions of dollars of damage to corporations worldwide. The folks at *Foreign Policy* also say that cyber warfare attacks risk "exposing the United States to blowback and turning the internet into a Wild West of hacking operations." However, cyber warfare may simply be required to combat America's enemies from now on.

Other jobs require coders to build programs that use AI and ML. These programs contain special models and algorithms that allow them to learn over time.

Simply put, there are thousands of different types of coding jobs available for people interested in working for or with the Department of Defense or the military!

SPECIAL DEPARTMENT OF DEFENSE AND MILITARY DIVISIONS FOR CODERS

Coders can be found throughout the Department of Defense, the military, and the contractors who work with them. But there are a few divisions that might be of particular interest to coders—especially those interested in the growing field of cybersecurity.

The US Army, Navy, Air Force, and Marines each have their own cyber divisions. These are called the US Army Cyber Command, the US Fleet Cyber Command, the Twenty-Fourth Air Force, and the Marine Corps Cyberspace Command, respectively. Within these divisions are smaller groups. For example, Army Cyber Command consists of the Army Network Enterprise Technology Command and the United States Army Intelligence and Security Command.

The Army Cyber Command, Fleet Cyber Command, Twenty-Fourth Air Force, and Marine Corps Cyberspace Command each have a similar stated mission. For example, the Army Cyber Command "integrates and conducts full-spectrum cyberspace operations, electronic warfare, and information operations, ensuring freedom of action for friendly forces in and through the cyber domain and the information environment, while denying the same to our adversaries." Similarly, the Twenty-Fourth Air Force delivers "full-spectrum, global cyberspace capabilities and outcomes for our service, the joint force and our nation."

These four military cyber divisions are part of a larger Department of Defense organization called the United States Cyber Command (USCYBERCOM). USCYBERCOM was formed in 2009 by US President Barack Obama to synchronize cybersecurity and cyber warfare efforts throughout the Department of Defense. Since then, USCYBERCOM has worked to shut down the cyber operations of America's enemies, such as the Islamic State (ISIS). It has also targeted Russian operatives who spread false information during the 2016 US election to sway the results.

In March 2018, USCYBERCOM announced it was taking a new approach to cyber warfare: "We have learned we must stop attacks before they penetrate our cyber defenses or impair our military forces, and through persistent, integrated operations, we can influence adversary behavior and introduce uncertainty into their calculations," the organization said. As part of this new approach the organization is working to develop what it calls the Unified Platform. This platform will enable cybersecurity specialists across USCYBERCOM to collaborate more easily. "Just as sailors rely on an aircraft carrier, pilots need airplanes or soldiers need tanks, cyber warriors require a system to … launch their attacks," says journalist Mark Pomerleau. "Pentagon leaders have said the Unified Platform will house offensive and defensive tools" and "allow for command and control, situational awareness and planning." To build this platform USCYBERCOM will need lots of talented coders!

USCYBERCOM is not the only division of the Department of Defense that relies on coders. Another is the Joint Artificial Intelligence Center (JAIC). This division was formed in 2018 to oversee AI efforts by almost all military and defense agencies.

Formed in 2009, USCYBERCOM synchronizes cybersecurity and cyber warfare efforts throughout the US Department of Defense.

JAIC's initial focus was on an effort called Project Maven. This involved a partnership with Google to develop AI software to sort and analyze images captured by drone cameras. Air Force General James Holmes explains the benefits of this technology: "It will free up people to focus on thinking about what they see and what it means in the intelligence field and on passing that information to decision-makers more [quickly]." As of this writing, however, the future of Project Maven is uncertain. Many Google employees protested the company's involvement in the project because the resulting technology could be used to identify and kill human targets. This prompted Google to withdraw from the project in June 2018.

Then there's the Defense Digital Service (DDS). Launched in 2015, the DDS operates like a tech startup company *inside* the Department of Defense. DDS joins coders in the military with coders from the tech industry to develop new technology for use in the military—a sort of "tour of duty for nerds," says division head Chris Lynch. The DDS's current focus is "developing drone-detection technologies, hunting adversaries on DoD networks, and redesigning training for cyber soldiers," says the division's website.

Finally, there are Department of Defense and military divisions that are more administrative in nature—many of which require the services of coders. One of these is the Defense Information Systems Agency (DISA). DISA employs enlisted personnel and civilians to provide information technology (IT) and communications support to various government leaders and agencies, including the Department of Defense and the military.

A FUTURE "CYBER FORCE"?

"The cyber domain will define the next century of warfare," Pentagon spokesperson Dana W. White said in May 2018. However, some experts worry that the US military may not be fully prepared for this challenge.

One key reason for this lack of readiness may be military culture. The military generally values "skills such as marksmanship, physical strength, the ability to leap out of airplanes and lead combat units under enemy fire," say Lieutenant Colonel Gregory Conti and Colonel John "Buck" Surdu—skills that are "irrelevant in cyber warfare." Worse, say Conti and Surdu, military culture may "inhibit and in some cases punish the development of the technical expertise needed for this new warfare domain."

Another reason for this lack of readiness is that the US government has been slow to develop clear policies for conducting cyber warfare. In 2010, the *Washington Post* reported that "Lawyers at the Justice Department's Office of Legal Counsel are struggling to define the legal rules of the road for cyber warriors." There has also been confusion about who should wage cyber warfare, the Department of

Students interested in coding can prepare for a career as a military coder. Here, young coders are taking part in the Hack the Air Force competition.

Defense and military or intelligence agencies like the Central Intelligence Agency (CIA) and the National Security Agency (NSA).

To address these and other problems, Conti and Surdu (among others) suggest creating a new military branch, called the US Cyber Force (USCF). "Adding an efficient and effective cyber branch," say Conti and Surdu, "would provide our nation with the capability to defend our technological infrastructure and conduct offensive operations." They continue: "Perhaps more important, the existence of this capability would serve as a strong deterrent for our nation's enemies."

"Deterring and responding to Russian hybrid warfare in cyberspace, countering Chinese cyber theft of US intellectual property, shutting down state and non-state actor attacks, defending American critical infrastructure—including the very machinations of our democracy, such as voting and political discourse and even cyber defense of US space assets," says one Washington think tank, "are just some of the heavy-lift missions that would occupy a US Cyber Force." If the US government does indeed form a Cyber Force, it will be a wonderful place for future coders to serve!

Computer camps are a great way to learn how to code. These coders are participating in Chrysler Automobile's technology day in 2018.

chapter_05

Starting Your Journey in Coding

If you're interested in working as a coder in the military or the Department of Defense, or for a military contractor, you can take steps now to prepare yourself. For example, you can use online tools to learn how to code (some especially for girls), enroll in computer science classes at your school, attend summer camps for coders, and more.

GETTING STARTED

After high school there are two paths to becoming a military coder. One is to enlist in the military. As an enlisted person, not only can you obtain the necessary training and knowledge to become a coder but you can also begin work in the field.

ETHICAL HACKERS AND "BUG BOUNTIES"

Some military coders work in the area of cybersecurity. One type of cybersecurity specialist is an ethical hacker.

An ethical hacker uses the same skills as a regular hacker to break into a computer system. The difference is that the ethical hacker does it to help an organization identify security flaws in the system—*not* to steal information from or damage the system.

The Department of Defense and the military use ethical hackers to ensure their systems are as secure as possible. There's even a program called Hack the Pentagon. This program is run by the Defense Digital Service. It gives prizes to ethical hackers who find bugs and other security flaws in Department of Defense systems—even if those ethical hackers don't work for the Department of Defense. In its first twenty-four days, this bug-bounty program uncovered 138 bugs. This persuaded the US Army, Navy, Air Force, and Marines to launch their own bug-bounty programs.

Whether you choose to work for the Department of Defense, military, or a military contractor, or you choose to remain on the outside but participate in bug-bounty programs, ethical hacking is a great option for coders!

The other path is to complete a college degree with a major in computer science. Then, with your degree in hand, you can apply to work for the Department of Defense or for a military contractor.

After you learn to code, you can obtain various professional certifications in specialty areas like application development and cybersecurity. These certifications help prove you are a capable coder.

CODING RESOURCES ON THE INTERNET

Before you can work as a military coder, you must learn how to code. There are loads of online resources to help you do that. Here are just a few resources:

CODE AVENGERS (HTTPS://WWW.CODEAVENGERS.COM): If you're interested in learning computer languages such as HTML, JavaScript, or Python, check out Code Avengers. This site offers online courses in these and other languages. Some of these courses are even offered for free!

CODECADEMY (HTTPS://WWW.CODECADEMY.COM): For online coding tutorials that offer easy-to-follow instructions and immediate feedback, visit Codecademy. As with Code Avengers, Codecademy offers some courses free of charge.

CODE.ORG (https://code.org):
Code.org doesn't just offer free online coding courses and project tutorials. It also develops coursework for schools to use for free.

KHAN ACADEMY (https://www.khanacademy.org/computing/computer-programming):
In the words of Khan Academy, "You can learn anything. For free. For everyone. Forever." This includes learning programming languages like JavaScript and HTML and studying topics like cryptology and algorithms.

SCRATCH (https://scratch.mit.edu):
This learning resource, offered by the Lifelong Kindergarten group at the Massachusetts Institute of Technology (MIT) Media Lab, is geared toward kids ages eight to sixteen and features tons of free tutorials and projects to teach coding concepts.

TYNKER (https://www.tynker.com):
Tynker caters to kids by offering self-paced, hands-on online courses. To start, you tinker with visual code blocks that represent fundamental programming concepts (hence the site's name). Then you progress to learning real programming languages like JavaScript and Python.

UDACITY (https://eu.udacity.com):
For more advanced coding resources—including classes on artificial intelligence and machine

learning and even building self-driving cars—kids (and adults) can check out Udacity.

CODING RESOURCES FOR GIRLS

Women currently hold just 24 percent of all jobs in computing. Incredibly, that number is likely to drop, as fewer than 1 percent of female college freshman say they plan to major in computer science. This explains why several organizations have formed in recent years to encourage girls to pursue a career in computer science by learning how to code. These are a few examples:

GIRLS WHO CODE (https://girlswhocode.com):
Girls Who Code was founded in 2012 to close the gender gap in technology by building a pipeline of future female coders. To that end, the organization has taught basic coding skills to more than ninety thousand girls across America and is "on track to achieve gender parity in computer science by 2027," says the organization's founder.

MADE WITH CODE (https://www.madewithcode.com):
Made with Code, which was launched by Google in 2014, combines online activities with real-world events to encourage girls to learn to code.

BLACK GIRLS CODE (http://www.blackgirlscode.com):
There are few female coders ... and even fewer female coders of color. The mission of Black Girls

Code is to change that. This effort involves a two-pronged attack: proving to the world that "girls of every color have the skills to become the programmers of tomorrow" and training "1 million girls by 2040."

SCHOOL CODING CLASSES

Experts predict that in the coming years coding jobs will be among the highest paid. You would think, then, that schools across America would offer coursework preparing students to work in this growing field. But few do. Indeed, according to a 2016 survey conducted by Google, just one in four schools teaches classes in computer programming. And many schools that *do* offer such classes don't count them toward graduation credit requirements—effectively discouraging students who are interested in coding from enrolling in coding classes.

If your school offers computer-programming classes, you should take them. They might not help you graduate, but they *will* help you prepare for a career as a military coder. If your school doesn't offer such classes, consider meeting with school administrators to persuade them to add some. When you do, you can tell them about nonprofit coding organizations like Code.org and CS First. Code.org offers free coding resources for schools, including curricula for grades K–12, workshops for teachers, and more. CS First, presented by Google, helps educators develop lesson plans

Computer classes in school are becoming more available. If you have the chance, take a class in coding!

in computer science and even provides free resource kits to support them in their efforts.

You could also join your school's computer club. These clubs usually meet after school. Members of computer clubs often work on projects designed to help them develop computer skills, including coding. They might also enter competitions called hackathons. In a hackathon, club members team up to build a functioning hardware device or software application. If your school doesn't have a computer club, think about starting one. This will probably mean partnering with a teacher or other adult at the school and completing a formal club application process. For help, check out CoderDojo.

These teenagers are being taught valuable coding techniques in a classroom.

This site offers online training for starting a computer club and provides free project guidelines.

You can also take instructor-guided coding classes outside school—either online or in person. For example, organizations like Code Wizards HQ and Coding with Kids offer online teacher-led classes. Another organization, called iD Tech, offers private teacher-led lessons online. If you'd rather take classes in person, check out establishments like Sylvan Learning and theCoderSchool, which offer classes after school and on weekends.

CODING CAMPS

Various organizations offer summer day camps to teach kids about coding, such as iD Tech and Codeverse. Some coding camps focus on cybersecurity. For example, NSA GenCyber Camps cater to kids in grades K–12 who are interested in both coding and cybersecurity. These camps, which are conducted at several sites nationwide and free of charge, are sponsored by the National Security Agency (NSA) and the National Science Foundation (NSF).

COLLEGE COURSEWORK AND MOOCs

Military coding jobs do not necessarily require a degree from a four-year college. It's possible to acquire the coding skills for these jobs in other ways—for example, by taking classes online or at a community college, or by joining the military and receiving the proper training there. But people who earn four-year college degrees in computer science will be more likely to secure higher-paying military coding jobs initially—especially Department of Defense jobs (rather than jobs within a specific military branch) and jobs with military contractors.

If you want to be a military coder whose specialty is cybersecurity, check out colleges and universities that support a special program called the Centers of Academic Excellence in Cyber Operations (CAE-CO). This program was

If you want to be a coder, you should invest time and money into earning a programming degree. There are many options to choose from.

developed by the NSA to prepare students for government cybersecurity jobs. To encourage students to enter CAE-CO (or similar) programs, the NSF and the Department of Homeland Security (DHS) have created a special scholarship called the Scholarship for Service. This scholarship pays up to $20,000 toward undergraduate studies. In exchange, people who accept this scholarship must commit to working for the US government in the area of cybersecurity for a set period of time—for example, in the Department of Defense or the military for five years.

In addition to offering classes for students who seek a degree, some colleges, universities, and other organizations offer online classes for nonstudents who simply want to learn about a particular subject. These are called massive online open courses (MOOCs). Many of these courses are free (although you may have to pay to earn a certification) and are often taught by seasoned professors. Some popular computer science MOOCs include Coursera Software Security, HarvardX Introduction to Computer Science, and Massachusetts Institute of Technology Introduction to Computer Science and Programming.

CERTIFICATIONS

Aspiring military coders can also earn professional certifications or credentials. This helps a person prove to prospective employers, such as military contractors, that they

Computer programmers work in 42, a specialized school for training aspiring computer coders.

know their stuff. Obtaining certifications or credentials usually involves taking a class and/or passing a skills test.

You can obtain certifications and credentials from various certifying organizations too. One of these is called CompTIA. It offers certifications in computer science fundamentals, cybersecurity, and other key IT areas. Another is the Institute of Electrical and Electronics Engineers (IEEE). It offers software development certification. Finally, Global Information Assurance Certification (GIAC) validates, or confirms, the skills of cybersecurity professionals. It's even possible to become a GIAC-certified ethical hacker!

In the end, it doesn't matter so much which route you take to learn how to code. What matters is that you gain the expertise necessary to build and maintain complex computer programs and systems. If you do that, you'll be well prepared to work as a military coder!

Glossary

algorithm A well-defined procedure that enables a computer to complete a task or solve a problem.

artificial intelligence (AI) The science and engineering behind "intelligent" machines.

autonomous Describes a machine or weapon that uses machine learning to "think" and act on its own.

big data Extremely large sets of data that can be analyzed to spot patterns and trends.

cloud computing The practice of storing and accessing data and programs over the internet.

compiler A computer program that translates source code written in a programming language into machine language.

cyber warfare A new type of warfare that involves breaking into an enemy's computer systems to spy, cause damage, or shut them down.

defense contractor A company or person that is hired by the Department of Defense or a branch of the military to build computer programs or other products. Defense contractors are also called military contractors or sometimes civilians.

drone An aircraft with no pilot inside. Some drones are used for surveillance. Other drones are used as weapons.

enlisted Describes someone who is a member of the military.

ethical hacking The practice of breaking into a computer system the same way a hacker does to help an organization identify security flaws in their computer systems.

hacker Someone who creates malware or uses a computer to gain unauthorized access to data.

machine language Language that a computer can read. Machine language consists of a series of zeroes and ones. The order in which these zeroes and ones appear in a computer program dictate how the program will behave.

machine learning (ML) The ability of a machine to learn through experience over time.

malware A type of computer program built by hackers to damage or exploit a computer system in some way.

open source Describes software whose source code is available to the general public to study or even modify.

platform Another word for a computer operating system. Examples of computer platforms include Microsoft Windows and Apple Macintosh.

precision weapon A weapon such as a missile that uses a computer to pinpoint its target.

reserve Describes someone who serves in the Army National Guard or the Air National Guard. Reserves work part-time and serve as backup for enlisted troops in the main military branches.

source code Computer program instructions that are written in a programming language.

trajectory The path and distance of a shell (or another object) after it is launched (as from a gun).

veteran Someone who once was but no longer is a member of the military.

Further Information

BOOKS

Briggs, Jason R. *Python for Kids: A Playful Introduction to Programming.* San Francisco: No Starch Press, 2012.

McCue, Camille. *Coding for Kids.* 2nd Edition. For Dummies. Hoboken, NJ: John Wiley & Sons, 2019.

Minnick, Chris, and Eva Holland. *JavaScript for Kids.* For Dummies. Hoboken, NJ: John Wiley & Sons, 2015.

Sande, Warren, and Carter Sande. *Hello World! Computer Programming for Kids and Other Beginners.* 2nd edition. Shelter Island, NY: Manning Publications, 2013.

Saujani, Reshma. *Girls Who Code: Learn to Code and Change the World.* New York: Viking Books for Young Readers, 2017.

WEBSITES
CYBER DEGREES

https://www.cyberdegrees.org/resources/security-clearances
The web page "A Quick Guide to Security Clearances" explains the ins and outs of obtaining a security clearance.

MILITARY.COM

https://www.military.com

This website connects members of America's military community with each other. In addition to sharing military news, it offers information about top military jobs—including coding.

MUSEUMS AND ORGANIZATIONS
THE COMPUTER HISTORY MUSEUM

http://www.computerhistory.org

Learn about the history of computers—and see a piece of the ENIAC machine—here.

MIL-OSS

https://mil-oss.org

The Military Open Source Software Group is a group within the Department of Defense that promotes the use of open source software within the Department of Defense and the military.

US DEPARTMENT OF DEFENSE

https://www.defense.gov

The US Department of Defense is in charge of defending the United States against attackers. The US Army, US Navy, US Air Force, and US Marine Corps are all part of the US Department of Defense.

BIBLIOGraPHY

Atherton, Kelsey. "The Pentagon Is Set to Make a Big
Push Toward Open Source Software Next Year." The
Verge, November 14, 2017. https://www.theverge.
com/2017/11/14/16649042/pentagon-department-of-
defense-open-source-software.

Bright, Peter. "Microsoft's Q# Quantum Programming Language
Out Now in Preview." Ars Technica, December 11, 2017.
https://arstechnica.com/gadgets/2017/12/microsofts-q-
quantum-programming-language-out-now-in-preview.

Byman, Daniel L. "Why Drones Work: The Case for
Washington's Weapon of Choice." Brookings Institution,
June 17, 2013. https://www.brookings.edu/articles/why-
drones-work-the-case-for-washingtons-weapon-of-choice.

Chabrow, Eric. "New Cyber Warfare Branch Proposed."
GovInfoSecurity, March 25, 2009. http://www.
govinfosecurity.com/blogs/new-cyber-warfare-branch-
proposed-p-160/op-1.

Computer Systems Programming. Airforce.com. Accessed
December 22, 2018. https://www.airforce.com/careers/
detail/computer-systems-programming.

Edwards, Paul N. *The Closed World: Computers and the Politics
of Discourse in Cold War America.* Cambridge, MA: MIT Press,
1997.

Ferdinando, Lisa. "Cybercom to Elevate to Combatant Command." US Department of Defense, May 3, 2018. https:// dod.defense.gov/News/Article/Article/1511959/cybercom- to-elevate-to-combatant-command.

Groll, Elias. "Trump Has New Weapon to Cause 'the Cyber' Mayhem." *Foreign Policy*, September 21, 2018. https:// foreignpolicy.com/2018/09/21/trump-has-a-new-weapon- to-cause-the-cyber-mayhem.

Gross, Grant. "U.S. Government Agencies Are Still Using Windows 3.1, Floppy Disks and 1970s Computers." *PC World*, May 25, 2016. https://www.pcworld.com/article/3075284/ hardware/us-government-agencies-are-still-using- windows-31-floppy-disks-and-1970s-computers.html.

Information Technology: Federal Agencies Need to Address Aging Legacy Systems. United States Government Accountability Office. Before the Committee on Oversight and Government Reform House of Representatives. (May 25, 2016) (testimony of David A. Powner, Director, Information Technology Management Issues). https://www. gao.gov/assets/680/677454.pdf.

Koerner, Brendan. "How the World's First Computer Was Rescued from the Scrap Heap." *Wired*, November 25, 2014. https://www.wired.com/2014/11/eniac-unearthed/.

McCammon, Sarah. "The Warfare May Be Remote but the Trauma Is Real." National Public Radio, April 24, 2017. https://www. npr.org/2017/04/24/525413427/for-drone-pilots-warfare-may-be-remote-but-the-trauma-is-real.

McIver, William J., Jr. "Computer Sciences: Social Impact." Encyclopedia.com, 2002. Accessed November 25, 2018. https://www.encyclopedia.com/computing/news-wires-white-papers-and-books/social-impact.

McManus, Doyle. "The Drone Warfare Drawbacks." *Los Angeles Times*, July 5, 2014. https://www.latimes.com/opinion/op-ed/la-oe-mcmanus-column-drones-20140706-column.html.

Mehta, Aaron. "DIUx, SCO Given Special Hiring and Contracting Authorities." Defense News, August 10, 2017. https://www. defensenews.com/pentagon/2017/08/10/diux-sco-given-special-hiring-and-contracting-authorities/.

Murray, Williamson. *America and the Future of War*. Stanford, CA: Hoover Institution Press, 2017.

Nakashima, Ellen. "Dismantling of Saudi-CIA Web Site Illustrates Need for Clearer Cyberwar Policies." *Washington Post*, March 19, 2010. http://www.washingtonpost.com/wp-dyn/content/article/2010/03/18/AR2010031805464_2. html?sid=ST2010031901063.

Newman, Lily Hay. "The Pentagon Opened Up to Hackers–And Fixed Thousands of Bugs." *Wired*, November 10, 2017. https://www.wired.com/story/hack-the-pentagon-bug-bounty-results.

Pappalardo, Joe. "The Air Force Will Treat Computer Coding Like a Foreign Language." *Popular Mechanics*, September 13, 2018. https://www.popularmechanics.com/technology/security/a23116594/air-force-coding-programming-language-mike-kanaan.

Pilkington, Ed. "Life as a Drone Operator: 'Ever Step on Ants and Never Give It Another Thought?'" *Guardian*, November 19, 2015. https://www.theguardian.com/world/2015/nov/18/life-as-a-drone-pilot-creech-air-force-base-nevada.

"SAGE: Semi-Automatic Ground Environment Air Defense System." MIT Lincoln Laboratory. Accessed December 19, 2018. https://www.ll.mit.edu/about/history/sage-semi-automatic-ground-environment-air-defense-system.

Schroeder, Dave, and Travis Howard. "Op-Ed: Time for a US Cyber Force." The Maritime Executive, August 31, 2018. https://www.maritime-executive.com/editorials/op-ed-time-for-a-u-s-cyber-force.

Serbu, Jared. "Impressed by DoD's Digital Service, Army Decides It Needs One of Its Own." *Federal News Network*, December 19, 2016. https://federalnewsnetwork.com/dod-

reporters-notebook-jared-serbu/2016/12/impressed-dods-
digital-service-army-decides-needs-one.

Tegmark, Max. "Autonomous Weapons: An Open Letter From AI &
Robotics Researchers." *Future of Life Institute*, July 28, 2015.
https://futureoflife.org/open-letter-autonomous-weapons.

Wallace, Mark. "How Software Is Eating the Military and What
That Means for the Future of War." *Fast Company*, July 5,
2017. https://www.fastcompany.com/40436077/how-
software-is-eating-the-military-and-what-that-means-for-the-
future-of-war.

Weisgerber, Marcus. "General: Project Maven Is Just the
Beginning of the Military's Use of AI." Defense One, June 28,
2018. https://www.defenseone.com/technology/2018/06/
general-project-maven-just-beginning-militarys-use-
ai/149363.

Work, Bob. "Remarks by Deputy Secretary Work on Third
Offset Strategy." U.S. Department of Defense, April 28, 2016.
https://dod.defense.gov/News/Speeches/Speech-View/
Article/753482/remarks-by-deputy-secretary-work-on-
third-offset-strategy.

Wunische, Adam. "AI Weapons Are Here to Stay." The National
Interest, August 5, 2018. https://nationalinterest.org/feature/
ai-weapons-are-here-stay-27862.

Index

ABOUT THE AUTHOR

Kate Shoup has written more than forty books and has edited hundreds more. When not working, Shoup loves to travel, watch IndyCar racing, ski, read, and ride her motorcycle. She lives in Indianapolis with her husband and their dog.